Phonetic Moods

Henry Arguelles

To Logan and Natalie: You two express more life and love than any poem could ever capture. Thank you for always being you.

Contents

Spark

On our date, I expected intense chemistry;
I wanted that passionate, burning flame
but when that didn't happen, I gave up on you;
I was selfish, immature, and lame.
I need to check my expectations
because I almost missed my mark;
I was so hung up on feeling a fire
that I didn't notice our spark.

The Things We Say

Maybe you told someone "forever"
and then split after a few years,
or promised them "I'll never hurt you"
then hurt them until they shed tears,
or maybe you swore "what's mine is yours"
then took what's yours away,
or told someone "you don't have to say sorry"
and refused to give them leeway,
or maybe you promised "I got your back"
and left them to fight alone,
or told someone "I'm here for you"
but sat back as they coped on their own;
perhaps you proclaimed "I believe in you"
but you really had some doubts,
or told someone "I'm not going anywhere"
when you wanted to get out;
you might have pledged "I'll never cheat"
and then promptly slept around;
you vowed "I'll always love you"
and then left when they were down.

I'm not here to judge you:
I've said some of those phrases too.
And I've heard them enough times
to recognize that they're usually untrue.

Too often in relationships
we don't give diligence to what we say;
maybe we should be more thoughtful with our words
instead of just repeating these clichés.

Read You

I see you popping up on my feed
and I'm tempted to see
just how different you are
now that you're not with me.

I'll admit that I've been curious
and have wanted to take a look;
let me go through your feed real quick
like I was skimming through a book.

After reading through your current story,
I'm not surprised by what I saw:
your pics and posts tell the tale of a person
that hasn't changed at all.

Yeah, you changed your hair
and you got another tattoo,
but those changes are only superficial:
did you work on the inner you?

I see nothing introspective in your chapters;
your words have no wisdom to be taught.
You've spent more time cultivating an image
than you did on your actual thoughts.

It doesn't seem like you're someone new;
you're the same person you were before.
Underneath the pictures you're still the same
and that's a shame: you could be so much more.

It never hurts to reread something but this time…
there wasn't anything new to discover.
You're still the same old book you were before;
all you did was change the cover.

Worth the Regret

During our first date,
I knew I was falling in love;
I'm worried it might be too soon
but I'm not gonna fret:
I know what I feel
and I'm willing to take a chance
and if we don't work out
you'll always be worth the regret.

The Onus of Communication

When the world doesn't understand you
and no one gets what you're trying to say,
the problem isn't everyone else:
it's that YOU need to find another way
to communicate what you want
if you ever want to be heard;
it's not on everyone else
to decipher your every word.

Parents Need to Grow Up Too

As parents we all think
that we know our kids
so damn well:
we (supposedly) know their every thought,
every fiber of their being,
down to every last little cell.
And because we raised them
we believe that our parenting
is always 100% correct,
so we take our relationship with them for granted
and rarely try
to actually connect
or to even really listen
when our kids try
to open up to us;
we shut them down when they communicate
because we swear we know what's best
and there's nothing else to ever discuss.

That is our fatal flaw
and why our kids later shun us
and become distant:
as they grow and gain independence
and become who they want
we become resistant.

We refuse to see them
as separate from us
and can't comprehend them as individual adults
that can change the plans
we laid out for them;
all we see are different results
that are not what we expected
based on who
we thought we knew;
we don't want our babies to change
and can't accept when our kids become humans
that are both familiar and new.

We need to accept and encourage our kids' growth
and let them be
who they want to be;
trust that you raised them right
and support them as they grow...
even if you don't always agree.

Romantic Optimism

Your secrets don't scare me
and neither does your past.

I appreciate you telling me about both
before I even asked.

Let's get past all that though,
and let's get over it fast;

I have a feeling about the two of us,
like this love is gonna last.

The Underlying Mechanics of a One-Night Stand

Meeting for drinks was fun;
we talked and flirted for hours;
we lost track of what happened last night...

Now we're both awake and in your bed;
you're looking at me with an awkward look,
and I'm feeling the need to take flight.

We didn't plan on a one-night stand:
We just got caught up in emotion and passion the night
before,
and the next day it was replaced with us feeling contrite.

Last night was fun, but we both know
that last night shouldn't have happened...
but we can't say that outright.

So I'll make up an excuse,
you'll pretend to believe it,
and we escape the awkwardness by being polite.

Time to Delete

If you're not ready to delete your ex's pics
from social media sites,
then you're not really ready to move on;
showing off old relationships ain't right.

Feel free to hold on to memories of your past:
those will always be your own.
But don't keep up pics that everyone can see
if you wouldn't have them up at home.

I Prayed Today

I don't know why but I
did something today
that I haven't done in years:
I prayed.

These past few months
have been incredibly tough,
and no matter what I've tried to make it better
it hasn't been enough.

So even though in God
I really don't believe,
I gave it a shot
and through prayer, tried to receive
a message of guidance
straight from the Lord,
but after a few minutes of halfhearted effort
I started to get bored.
Feeling foolish, I cursed myself
for stooping so low:
as an educated and rational human why would I pray
to a being that no one could prove to know?

I got up, passed a mirror,
and in my reflection all I could see
was a bitter, cynical, and arrogant man
that refused to even potentially believe

in anything and everything
he couldn't comprehend,
and was so defensive and insecure about everything
he'd never let anyone or anything in.

Still unsure, I tried to pray again -
to really talk to God -
openly, plainly, without formal prayer;
I didn't want to be a fraud.

As I was talking/praying,
I realized I had no clue
about how I should live
or what I should do,
and that after all the things that
lately I had been through,
I felt so empty and lonely:
I had no one else to turn to.

The more I prayed, the better I felt:
I really thought God was listening, and I felt hope,
so, I asked for some sort of divine sign...
and did I get one?

Nope.

I didn't get an answer or miracle
or any type of reply,
but I did get something
I didn't realize I'd been missing inside:

by letting go of my pride
and acknowledging the possibility
that there could be something I didn't understand above me...
I finally learned humility.

After praying, I learned to let go
of the idea that my knowledge is the be-all and end-all
and that accepting something greater than me
won't be my downfall.

I didn't want to pray,
but I'm ready to concede
that I didn't get what I asked for
but I got what I truly did need.

After praying, my head hangs lower and
my stance is less aggressive,
but I see much more than I ever did
and the future doesn't feel so oppressive.

I'm not ready to call myself a believer just yet
but that's ok: you don't have to be devout
to open up and be changed by a power higher than you:
that's what prayer is all about.

Books (and everything else)

Read through all the pages
and sure,
there might be something more...
but sometimes
it's ok to judge a book by its cover:
that's what they're there for.

Always on My Phone

I'm very technologically connected;
I'm on a total of 16 different apps combined.
I'm constantly checking to see if someone messaged me,
no matter the place, occasion, or time.

I guess you're right to say
I spend a lot of time on my phone,
but that doesn't mean I'm addicted to it;
I just don't know how to be alone.

Silver Lining

This is the first night
I didn't tell you good night
but it's also the first night
we didn't have a fight.

We Just Met

We just met and you're offering me the moon
and the stars in the sky
but it's much too soon
to take off and fly
high into this potential love
that you say you've found;
I've already lived in castles above and
this time I'm keeping my feet on the ground.

Try Some Introspection

Why do you keep contacting me?
You need to introspect your id:
Figure out and get over yourself;
I already did.

Forgive and Forget

Holding on to memories of us
was, for a long time, a necessity:
I couldn't process it all so
I needed you as my enemy;
I had to remain a victim
and hold on to my anger at you
because that's what helped me
get through the loss of the life I knew.
But I've spent too much time
trying to reminisce and relive -
it's toxic and has held me back;
I need to move on and forgive.
By choosing to let go of my pain
I'm choosing to live and let go of regrets,
and now that I've let myself forgive you,
I'm finally ready to forget.

Don't Take It Personally

My love, please don't ever tell me again
"Don't take it personally."

I'd prefer:

"It wasn't intentional;"
"The words came out wrong;"
"It was a bad joke;"
"I meant something else."

But don't tell me not to take things personally.

We are in a relationship;
it's nothing but personal.

I Have Been a Stubborn Man

I have been a stubborn man,
never admitting I was wrong;
I thought I always had to be right
to show that I was strong.

What an ignorant way to live,
thinking I knew all there was to know;
I swore I was infallible
when I really needed to grow.

Because of that I argued a lot
and pushed people away;
I was dismissive whenever
someone disagreed with what I had to say.

It's too late to make amends –
burned bridges can't be rebuilt –
so in exchange for being humbled
I must always carry the guilt
that I was such an asshole
that always refused to listen;
I didn't understand that compromise
was more powerful than attrition.

Not So Happy Alone

As a single introvert
I'm happy to be by myself
but when the loneliness is oppressive

I wish I was alone with someone else.

Self-Respect

You text me at 3,
wanting to come around;
I've always let you in
but tonight I'm turning you down.

I love you so much that
I took whatever from you I could get,
but I'm tired of us together
being something I later regret.

A Summary of (some...maybe most of) My Relationships

The way you look:
flawless.
The way we make love:
rawness.
Every moment with you:
timeless.
The reasons we fell apart:
madness.
What we wanted to give each other:
happiness.
What we were left with:
bitterness.
What we never learned to offer:
forgiveness.

Perspective

I was wrong when
I broke your heart, and
I don't deserve
for you to ever
forgive;
but just know
that what went around
came back around
and I can finally understand
your perspective.

Homebody

I proudly call myself a homebody:
I don't need or want to go out
because here at home with you
I have everything I can't live without.
Sure, there's a lot out there
that might be exciting to see,
but I already live the greatest adventure
here, in our home, with you next to me.

Just A Fling

"Come over and let's chill"
you texted me tonight;
you're lonely and want me to thrill
your body because I can't fight
how much you mean to me
and how much I love you...
it hurts that you can't see me
as more than just a screw.
I have feelings that are complex -
I need more than just the physical.
I want more with you than just sex;
I want a connection that's inimitable.
And every time I voice that thought
you tell me not to worry about a thing,
but I guess it's my fault I'm in this spot;
I settled for just being a fling.

Single Parenting/Dating

Finding new romance can be a lot of fun
but it's a game single parents can't play:
we don't want to waste our time
with someone not ready for commitment someday.

Casual dating isn't our thing because
introducing someone to our kids is hard,
so If we date, please be sure you're ready for reality:
bad breakups leave more than just us grownups scarred.

You Can't Say I Changed

I never put up a front,
never lied about who I am;
laid out everything I am to you
because I wanted you to understand
that I could never be
someone else's fantasy.

All I ever promised you is
that I would always be me.

Modern Relationship Goal

It would be nice
to find someone
to share my life;
hopefully she'd be willing
to be my wife.

If not...

A monogamously committed and
non-legally binding cohabitation based on
equity, trust, communication, and love
would be great too.

Parenting

Someone once told me
that I was a good parent,
and that kind of bothered me
even though I knew what the person meant.
And what bothered me about it
is that they didn't see
that what makes me a good parent
has very little to do with me.

Parenting isn't easy
but it's easy with a child like you;
when problems came up,
together we figured out what to do.
And when I felt overwhelmed
it was your trust in me that got me through
some impossibly hard times
when I didn't have a clue.
You showed wisdom beyond your age
and suggested we try something new
and even when I thought it wouldn't work
somehow...you knew.

If I am a good parent
there's only one reason why:
it's because in this life I was blessed
that you, my child, are mine.

Missed the Moon While Counting the Stars

I was too focused on looking
for what I expected
that I never saw the love you gave
and so I rejected
the way you showed me love
because it was not exactly like my own;
I can only see all that you offered me
now that I'm alone.

Neighbor

The old lady
in the apartment across from me
died a week ago.

She died lonely.

The fact that she died alone hit me hard
and I wondered who was to blame:
herself? Family that abandoned her? Maybe me
for never even knowing her name.

Love is Just a Feeling

I've thought before that love can conquer all,
just like people say...
but love didn't buy us food
as we were waiting for pay day.
Love wasn't enough to overcome
long-distance and issues with parental custody
so that two people couldn't live together
even if it was our destiny.
And how did love resolve our
differences with religion and politics?
It didn't at all, because
its supposed power cannot fix
all the incompatibilities that
a couple may share;
just because you love someone
doesn't mean that life will care
about the love you feel
and how it's supposed to conquer all;
the more impossible power you ascribe to love
the further you will fall
into a hole of unrealistic expectations
and unsubstantiated beliefs;
if love is the only answer to one's troubles...
how can you ever find relief?

Sometimes we stall in our relationships
and have trouble moving forward again,
but you can't just have faith in love
and ignore what's up ahead.

I know it may not be sexy
or romantic or magical,
but for a relationship to last
it has to also be practical.

Right Song, Wrong Time

I knew when we met that we couldn't work;
our lives can't be compromised.
And even though I had steeled myself
I'll admit I was surprised
at how much it hurt
knowing I'd never hold you again
and that the most we'd ever be
to each other is just friends.
The promise of future happiness was lost
because I gave up on it too soon;
I never got to dance with you
underneath a harvest moon.

Or Maybe I Just Crave Drama?

I've been wondering for a while
if you'd show up;
haven't heard from you at all
since our breakup.
I keep thinking you'll be
waiting at my door
or that we'll bump into each other
at the grocery store.
I know I don't love you:
of that I'm sure...
but the desire to see you
holds a very strong allure.
I know I crave some drama
but this is something more:
why do I want to see you
when I ran from you before?
But you're not pursuing me
in any way at all...
so why do I keep hoping
to at least get a telephone call?
I've thought about it a lot
and I guess I just want to be
as memorable to you
as you are to me.

Not Your Fault

I once broke the heart
of the kindest soul
because I lacked the strength
to let them go.
My doubts and fears
wouldn't let me commit
to a future together
even when they wouldn't quit
on the idea of "us"
and a life filled with love and laughter;
in the end I was too cynical to believe
in happily ever after.

Post-Relationship Truth #1

No matter what you do in life
or who you're with next,
to someone you will never be more
than just another ex.

Post-Relationship Truth #2

Even if takes years
until your new partner is found,
during all that time that passed
you were technically on the rebound.

All I Want (Now)

I once went crazy
for painted red lips
and I used to lust
after swaying hips
but now...

I just want someone
to sing in the car with.

Some Thoughts on Suicide

We can't think about suicide
as a way out for cowards;
if someone feels that despondent...
it was probably the only time they felt empowered.
Too often, we're quick to dismiss
the decisions people are driven to make
instead of trying to understand
what would lead them to make
such a drastic and final choice
as ending their own life;
we need to reach out and help those in need
find hope and overcome their strife.
So please, don't be in a rush to judge
those that have lost all hope-
try to understand their reasoning
and why they were unable to cope.
Life is really hard sometimes,
and going through pain everyday can feel like a chore,
so if you know someone on the edge, lend a hand and
remember:

You yourself have probably considered suicide before.

Zen (Not Romance)

Lately I have all this energy
to get things done:
been finishing up projects
I'd forgotten I'd begun.
I'm more mindful now
of the path I want to take
and I've been working so hard,
I don't want this momentum to break.
I keep moving forward
and this feeling is new:
a sense of personal accomplishment
that I never really knew.
And I'm not so moody
now that I'm on my own:
no one to fight with
so I'm forced to personally grow.
I finally feel a sense of purpose
with where I belong in society:
I feel more comfortable out there
and not always wracked with anxiety.
I guess I'm ready get back out there
and start dating once again
but I don't think it's worth
disrupting my feeling of Zen;
now that my heart
is finally on the mend,
I'm not in a rush
to get it broken again.

Timing

I finally met "the One"
but we didn't last long
and the reason for that
was that our timing was wrong.

A lifetime of searching
and it doesn't seem fair
that when it comes to love,
Life doesn't care.

Money Isn't Everything, But...

No, money can't buy happiness
but let's be real:
when you have bills up to your neck
there's no way
to be happy living
paycheck-to-paycheck.

Keeping It Real

We all want to be better after a breakup,
to move on, grow, and evolve.
But no matter what we do,
some feelings stay unresolved.
That's why we secretly wish
to run into our exes on the street:
so they can see how wonderful we're doing
and for them to feel regret when we meet.
Yeah, sure: we moved on
and truly do wish them well...
but a little part of us wants them to suffer;
we're all petty as hell.

Long-Distance Dating

I don't want to live my life like this,
being with someone some of the time;
I want to be by your side
and have you next to mine.
I know our lives are complex
and we need to compartmentalize
but doing that isn't want I want for us;
at our age time flies
and soon we'll be too old
and our hair's already turning gray...
I want to be with you all the time
and not just every few days.
I love you but I can't do this:
I want us to share a home
and if that can never happen
then I'd rather be alone
because I already live a life
that's mostly independent
and my love for you
isn't stronger than my resentment
at the way the universe
won't just let us be;
no matter what our future holds
I know I'll still be lonely.

Gambling

I've been mocked for not gambling much,
and that's fair, to a degree:
taking reckless chances with my money
never held much appeal to me.
And love is so fickle and unknowable
that when it comes to playing I often choose to not;
the odds are always against you,
whether you wager a little of yourself or a lot.
That's why when I do actually gamble,
it's only for the highest stakes:
I gamble on myself
and the choices that I make.
When I bet on myself and succeed
I know that my faith in the risk was true,
but when I gamble on myself and lose,
that makes me a loser times two.

Exes Aren't Always Totally Evil

I know you think our time together
was like a punishment or curse,
but I swear that it was never my intention
to make your life worse.
People should be happy in relationships
every chance they get;
I know I was difficult and
got off on being upset.
I'm sorry that I caused you
so much drama and grief;
I hope you're happy now:
you deserve to find peace.

Analyzing My Argumentative Nature

When people
(like me)
always have to argue,
it's not because we're strong;

it's just a lot easier
to insist we're right
than to acknowledge
we might be wrong.

Sundays

Everyone loves Sundays,
but for me they're bittersweet,
because at the end of almost every Sunday
my heart is no longer complete.

I have my kids most weekends, and
when they're with me I feel whole,
but when they're gone I'm lonely and
unable to be consoled.

This cycle has been going on for years
and yet, I still can't believe
that our time together isn't infinite
and it always hurts on Sundays when they leave.

As they get older and live their lives
I expect my sadness will be less,
but as long as they leave on Sunday nights
I'll always be a mess.

Why I Look at You How I Do

I knew I loved you the moment I met you
and every day I feel my love grow
but I've been mistaken in love before
so I need to take it slow
and make sure it's not infatuation
or a silly little crush
because my pattern seems to be
to always be in a rush
and go from dating to forever
without understanding what I feel;
too much of me being in love with love
and not seeing what was real.

I know you might be waiting
for me to say "it" first,
but I'm scared of being a fool again;
that feeling is the worst.

I'm sorry that I've closed myself off
when in the past I was more open;
too many discarded relationships
have left me a little broken.

I feel compelled to be stoic
and restrain myself from going all out,
but I can't stop my eyes from saying
the words I won't let out.

Someone Else's Fault

I know I have an unknown enemy;
I don't know if it's a jealous coworker or a vindictive ex.
Whoever it is, they are relentless, because
they work nonstop to make sure my life is wrecked.
Maybe it's no person – maybe it's God himself -
that's been behind my suffering for so long?
Because I can't understand why;
I've never, ever, ever, ever, ever done anything wrong.
No one has ever suffered what I have suffered,
and no one has gone through as much pain as me…
I wonder…could it all be my fault? No way:
taking responsibility for my life would be too easy.

No Momentum

I thought that at this point in my life
I would finally be able to thrive,
but things keep getting harder and harder;
I want to do more than just survive.

Meandering Musings

You worry that your thoughts meander
but I think they're divine;
you have a unique way of thinking
and I get excited when you share your mind.
Don't worry that you're rambling
and don't try to focus on one thing to say;
just muse on and on please:
I could listen to you talk all day.

Tired

I'm tired:

Tired of lying all the time
about how I really feel,
tired of feeling pain
from wounds that don't heal,
tired of arguing
with the people I love,
and tired of looking
for a sign from up above.

I just want to sleep for a bit
and let my soul rest,
because I'm so damn tired of feeling
like not waking up might be best.

Self-Reflection #4

I can't spend every single fight
trying to establish my might;
I need to learn how to be contrite
because I always think I'm right.

Self-Reflection #5

I'm always a mess
when I become single again,
and I tend to put my new partner though hell.

That's not fair to them
because the problem is me:
I never learned to take rejection well.

Dreaming About My Ex

I intermittently dream about my ex
even though we've long been through.
The dreaming seems to start again
whenever I meet someone new.

My subconscious is trying to talk to me
but I ignore it, so at night it shouts:
"you're not in love with your new person
if it's your ex you dream about!"

Not Really Ready, But...

I just broke up,
gotta start dating again-
my life is lonely;
I don't have any friends.
At night all I have
are the thoughts in my head;
that's why I rush to find
someone to share my bed.

Breaking Up a Little Differently This Time

Usually, the dumper tells the dumpee
"it's not you, it's me"
in an effort to be polite,
because they don't want to cause pain
and would rather feel contrite.
In our case, though,
I don't want to be so kind.
You're not who I thought you were
and I need you out of sight and mind.
To hell with being nice
because I need this to be through!

You don't deserve to be with me;
it's not me: it's YOU.

Pride Before The Fall

The stupidest thing I ever did
was not talk to you for weeks
because I didn't want to give in
and seem like I was weak.
I rejected your attempts
to try and make things right;
you wanted to move forward
and I just wanted to win the fight.
So much damage done
trying to stand tall...
I was too wrong to be humble;
my pride needed to fall.

Everything Looks Fine...

Take off those rose-colored glasses
once in a while,
even if it seems like a drag;
if you leave them on too long
you probably won't notice
someone's red flags.

Just Listen

I really want to talk to you
because I have so much on my chest
and we love each other so much
that I know I can count on you when I'm stressed.
But sometimes, I just need you to listen
and hear what I have to say,
because the simple act of just listening
helps me feel like things will be ok.
So, for right now, I don't need advice
or suggestions on what I should do
and please don't tell me
about a similar experience you went through.
And no matter how much you believe in one,
don't share with me a platitude,
because they're just so trite and dismissive
there's no way they'd improve my mood.
And trust me: I know that others have stood
where I'm currently at before,
but citing the frequency and statistics of my problems
is not what I'm asking you for.
I'm not asking you for all that not-so-helpful stuff,
but I know your desire to help is sincere,
so save it, please; all I need from you is
to just listen and lend me an ear.

Self-Image

Every day
I try to be
the person I want to be,
but when I look in the mirror
all I see
is what people think of me.

Why I'm Quiet

I know I don't talk a lot;
I hate the sound of my own voice.
And I've always suffered from shyness
so my quietness isn't always by choice.
I also stutter sometimes
when I'm excited about what I want to say,
but when I feel comfortable and secure,
I'll ramble on all day.
I never want you to think
that when you talk I'm quiet because I don't care;
I'm quiet because I'm so worried about sounding stupid
and it's hard to get over being scared.
Give me some time
and I'll come out of my shell,
because with you I really want
to talk, sing, laugh, and YELL!

And when I finally do, please let me talk
and really listen to my words,
because I don't always talk a lot
but I always want to feel like I'm heard.

Just Some Advice

Watch out for potential partners
that demand to be pursued;
they'll put themselves up on a pedestal
but will never do the same to you.

Reflection on Dating #4

The current routine for me
upon becoming single again:
sign up for a dating app, take horrible selfies,
try to set up a clever profile and then
start swiping on other's profiles
and get excited when someone swipes me back,
but that begins
the getting-to-know-you texting and chat
that goes mundanely pleasant enough for us to meet-
usually somewhere safe
like a public park
or a generic café.
And that first meeting/date is usually bland enough
and there's nothing glaringly wrong...
until I start checking the time on my phone
and wondering how long
I have to stay
before I politely leave,
and when I finally leave, I sigh in relief
because this time I didn't leave my heart on my sleeve.
I felt, early on, this date had no future
and neither did the ones before,
and after each one I can feel cynicism setting in
because finding love has become a chore.
And as I go through the routine, I always say
"Love and me are through!"
Because it's been far too long since I felt really nervous
about getting to know someone new.

Online Dating

People holding up some fish;
people acting like their rich;
lots of filtered pics
or photos taken in '06;
profiles that reveal no humanity
or words that show the writer's insanity...

It's hard dating through apps:
people rarely reveal what they're like inside,
and the more first (and last) dates I have,
the more virtual romance leaves me dissatisfied.

Snap

Everyone thinks
I've got things under control,
that I'm doing well
and just letting things roll
off my back
like they're no big deal
and that during this difficult time
I'm focusing on myself to heal,
but the truth is that I'm not ok.

At all.

In fact, I'm worried
I'm about to fall
into a cycle of depression
and self-harm,
and if I showed anyone my true feelings
they'd definitely be alarmed.
I know I seem fine to everyone
but I don't have any more hope to tap,
and if things don't change soon...

I'm gonna snap.

Face Value

You don't need to know
every single thought inside my mind
and if you could search inside my brain
you might not like all that you'd find,
so don't stress over everything I think
and instead judge me for what I do;
it's my actions that should prove my love
and that should be enough for you.

Leave Already

My door is right in front of you:
same way you came in
is the same way you get out.
Stop talking about it
and just go already;
this drama I can live without.

Maybe I'm Not Ready Yet

I've worked so hard
to achieve some stability
and to ensure that my life
has some sense of tranquility;
I'm scared to let someone in, because
they could hurt me and end all that easily.
So, no matter how emphatically
the next person may beg and plea,
I don't think I'll ever let anyone
get close enough to see
all that I keep hidden
deep inside of me.

Accepting Your Partner

Relationships don't end
because people change:
they fail because
we expect people to stay the same.
You can't just love the person
for who they are today:
you have to be willing to love
who they might be the next day.
Nothing in this world is static and
everyone must change and grow;
accept someone completely
and they'll be there tomorrow.

Sleeping With You

When I can't fall asleep
because of incessant anxieties in my head,
only one thing helps me sleep:
cuddling up and falling asleep with you in bed.
I feel relaxed and calm
with you laying next to me,
and knowing that when I wake up you'll be there
lets me fall asleep with peace and security.
Sometimes, you playfully chide me
for falling asleep right away, but
of course I fall asleep quickly:
with you I can't wait to start each day.

Just Some Whining

Love sucks,
it's trite,
and no one will ever
get it right.

Don't mind me:
I'm just in a mood.

With no one here next to me,
I have too much time to brood
about how my exes
so quickly moved on,
while I stay here at home
sullen and withdrawn.

If I was currently in love
I'd feel differently, I know,
but I think I'm just bitter
because no one regrets letting me go.

Relationship Dynamics #1

You say you've been hurt before
and now you need proof
that I'm different than the others in your past
and that I'll always tell the truth.

I totally get that, because
lying is something we both can do without;
but what I need from you is assurance that
you'll always give me the benefit of the doubt.

It seems like trust is an issue for us both,
since past relationships caused us both heartache,
so let's agree to move past that now
and not punish each other for another's mistake.

Not Lonely, Maybe Depressed, Definitely Sad

The sun is shining,
people are outside playing...
but I feel so alone and sad
and I just feel like staying
in bed, hidden away,
tucked away under the blanket;
I wish everyone in the world would go away
but they won't, so the sadness I have to tank it
and put on a happy face
for everyone's sake
because they can't handle the truth:
that my smile is fake.
I don't really know
why I feel this way
but no matter what positive things happen to me,
the sadness grows deeper with each new day.
I wonder sometimes
if I'm feeling depressed
but I have no reason to be:
people tell me all the time that I'm blessed
and that I have no right
to feel like this,
as if I'm choosing this mysterious aching inside
over happiness and bliss.
I guess they're right
and it'll go away on its own...
but if all these people around me are so right, then
why do I feel so alone?

Just Say Whatever It Is

Sometimes we don't say
what we need to express
and the act of holding it in
leaves us an emotional mess
and that mess disrupts
every element of our lives
and since we won't reveal the truth
we cover it with lies
and as we maintain our silence
we brood and dwell
and we think we're keeping a secret

but everyone can tell

that there's something wrong
that we refuse to let out;
some things are just too loud
to be silent about.

Letting Go

Don't waste hope
on someone that left;
it's not worth you
getting all stressed.
It may feel right now
like they're the one that got away
but if that were true...
they would have wanted to stay.
Let the past go and
for your own sake, move on.
Don't try to get someone back
that wants to be gone.

Not Again

When our relationship was over
you were determined to see it end;
now you're trying to get back in my life
crying about what we had back then,
but I'm sorry that I can't go back:
my heart is finally on the mend
and I'll never give you another chance
to break my heart again.

Memories

I have no photos left of us
and there's no trace online or anywhere;
it's not because I hate you and
it's not because I didn't care.

I still have every memory
from when we broke up to when we met
so I don't need to constantly remember
the one person I can't forget.

I Know; I've Done It Twice

If you really think
that marriage will solve everything,
then your relationship is doomed
before you ever put on that ring.

Détente

We ignore each other,
we don't talk
or even text;
we eat separate meals,
we sleep in separate rooms...
we don't even bother with pretext.

It's been like this
for days and days...
maybe even weeks;
both of us
too damn prideful
to ever seem meek.

For all I know
you could be dying or dead
alone in our bedroom.
All I have to do to
is just reach out...
but I'd rather just assume
that you're ok
and we'll fix things
because our love is strong
but...
if we really love each other
why do we dwell on who's more wrong?

This constant cycle
of passion and fighting...
let's not do this anymore.
You and I
need to learn to compromise
and end our stupid war.

Please Stop Growing Up

When my kids were younger
we'd read together, watch movies,
and play games all the time,
but they're getting older
and they don't want to hang out with me as much
because they want more of their own personal time.

I'm trying not to be sad, because
I know it's not deliberate –
just a result of growing up;
I'm having a hell of a time though
coming to terms with the fact
that soon they'll be grownups.

Every so often, though
they forget to be mature
and they act like kids again.
And I'm ecstatic until the moment's over
and I'm faced with the truth
that they'll never be little again.

Unmanly

I didn't know how to be a man
that was secure and complete;
to compensate for my fragility
I would fight and I would cheat
and because I thought
that anyone could be replaced,
I ended up being what I feared most:
an absolute disgrace.

Shortcomings

We both put our all in
but in your own way you put in more;
you weren't always easy to talk to
but I refused to build a rapport.
Our life had ups and downs
and when it finally got too rough,
I looked for a way out
because I thought you weren't enough.
It was easier to leave you
than to turn to you for support;
I blamed you for our shortcomings
but it was I who came up short.

I'm Not Pieces

I have been loved in pieces-
disseminated and picked apart-
and I don't think that was fair
because from the very start
I presented myself transparently,
and not just my best parts;
I deserve to be complete
in someone else's heart.

Optimistic (ish)

Life will give you problems
and then it'll give you more
and sometimes it gets to the point
where just being awake feels like a chore
and at that point you get despondent
and filled with worry and doubt
and there often doesn't seem to be
any good way out
of the hole you're in-
it seems to keep going down-
and when you try and ask for help
you find there's no one around.

I know what it feels like
when life treats you viciously
and you feel constantly attacked
and what you need is empathy.

I don't have any solutions for that
and I won't offer false hope;
all I can say is take it one day at a time
and hold on while you cope.
And if you can't make it
from one day to the next,
then go from hour to hour
if that works best.

Or minute to minute
or from one moment to another;
worry about what works for you
and not what others

say is right
or say that you need to try;
be honest with yourself
and if you need to cry
there's nothing wrong with that
because pain is real
and only by allowing its expression
can you ever really heal.

Life will suck sometimes
and sometimes it'll be great
and for every moment you love
there will be two that you hate
but those moments that inspire you,
those count for double,
and will (hopefully) carry you
through any trouble.

And if they don't,
and if you start to fret,
take a minute and consider this:

the sun hasn't stopped rising yet.

Thank you for taking the time to read these poems; hopefully you found something in them that resonates with your life.

Feel free to contact me at:

henryarguelles@gmail.com

https://twitter.com/henry_arguelles

www.ingramcontent.com/pod-product-compliance
Lightning Source LLC
Chambersburg PA
CBHW031538040426
42445CB00010B/591